TIMELINES IN SCIENCE

SCIENCE OF THE ANCIENT WORLD

Craig Boutland

ROSEN PUBLISHING

Published in 2025 by The Rosen Publishing Group, Inc.
2544 Clinton Street, Buffalo, NY 14224

Portions of this work were originally authored by Charlie Samuels and published as *Ancient Science*. All new material in this edition was authored by Craig Boutland.

PICTURE CREDITS
t=top, b=bottom, l=left, r=right, c=center

Front Cover: Shutterstock: Millionstock.com b, Stephen Seibel tl, Whatafoto tr, WitR tc.
Inside: Ablestock: 58; iStockphoto: Tom Brakefield 49, Tobias Helbig 48, Hemera 20, 23t, Vladimir Piskunov 40t, Maria Toutoudaki 29t; Public Domain: Thinkstock/Photos.com 15, 22, 24, 25, 29b, 34, 36, 46, 47t, 47b, 50, 51t, 52, 53; Shutterstock: Francisco Javier Ballester 19, Baloncici 40b, Paul Banton 60t, W. H. Chow 30, JB Coleto 11, Louise Cukrov 39, Gorodenkoff 7, Images Talk 59b, Janprchal 37, Doctor Kan 27cr, Jin Yang Lee 17, maradon333 12, Pavle Marjanovic 18, Luciano Mortula 35, Erick N 41, Nejron Photo 21, Mikhail Olykainen 14, Sang H. Park 26, Pedarilhos 10, PhotoChur 13, Polartern 61, Nicolas Primola 8, Michael Rosskothen 43, David H. Seymour 5, P Titpong 9, Aleksander Todorovic 28, Olga Utlyakova 38, Alexandr Vasilyev 23b, Wlad74 6, Sybille Yates 27tl.

All other artwork and illustrations Brown Bear Books Ltd

Cataloging-in-Publication Data

Names: Boutland, Craig.
Title: Science of the ancient world / Craig Boutland.
Description: Buffalo, NY : Rosen Young Adult, 2025. | Series: Timelines in science | Includes glossary and index.
Identifiers: ISBN 9781499477641 (pbk.) | ISBN 9781499477658 (library bound) | ISBN 9781499477665 (ebook)
Subjects: LCSH: Discoveries in science–History–Juvenile literature. | Science–History–Juvenile literature.
Classification: LCC Q180.55.D57 B68 2025 | DDC 509–dc23

Manufactured in the United States of America

CPSIA Compliance Information: Batch #CSRYA25.
For further information, contact Rosen Publishing at 1-800-237-9932.

CONTENTS

Introduction

It is easy to see science as being very modern. In fact, the desire to understand the world and to develop technological improvements is as old as humankind.

The earliest humans learned to use stones as tools to make other tools or weapons from wood or bone. The domestication of plants and animals allowed people to settle in communities and grow crops, rather than moving around to hunt game or collect wild plants. Recorded history began with the invention of writing. People wrote down events; they also developed numbers to keep records of farm animals, grain, or trade. To keep track of the seasons, they devised calendars based on the study of the stars and the moon: astronomy.

The Classical Age

The first people we identify with science, and whose names we know, were Greek philosophers, such as Aristotle and Archimedes. They applied a systematic approach to collecting knowledge. The Greeks were also highly practical, and applied their knowledge to architecture. The same process was continued by the Romans, who built great aqueducts for water supply and thousands of miles of roads.

About This Book

This book focuses on the development of science and technology from the earliest period of human history through the classical age of ancient Greece and Rome to about 500 CE. It contains two different types of timelines. Along the bottom of each page is a timeline that covers the whole period. It lists key events and developments, color-coded by category. Most of the chapters also have a specific timeline, running vertically down the sides of the pages. This timeline provides more specific details about the particular subject of the chapter. Because of the lack of written records for much of the period covered by this book, most of the dates are estimates.

The Greeks applied systematic knowledge to practical skills such as architecture. The Parthenon in Athens was built to give the appearance of perfect proportion: the columns actually taper toward the top.

Stone and Wooden Tools

Humans have been using tools for hundreds of thousands of years. Early stone tools were used to hunt and skin animals, as well as to make shelters and clothes.

It is thought that stone was first used to make tools about 3.3 million years ago. During the Stone Age, a "hammerstone" was used to make tools such as axes, small hand-shaped rocks, wooden spears, and clubs. The hammerstone was hit against other pieces of stone to shape them into tools. Small pieces of rock that broke off were used as spearheads or arrowheads.

Survival

Early humans had to compete for food with large, dangerous predators such as lions, bears, and hyenas. Tools were essential for human survival. Modern humans, *Homo sapiens*, appeared in Africa about 200,000 years ago. From about 75,000 years ago, *Homo sapiens* began to spread throughout the world. By this time, humans had developed a wide range of tools.

A typical hand ax. This stone has been shaped to be held comfortably.

TIMELINE

1,000,000 BCE –80,000 BCE

KEY:

Engineering and Technology

1,000,000 BCE Human ancestors (*Homo erectus*) use hammers made from antlers to create other tools for cutting, drilling, and shaping.

750,000 BCE *Homo erectus* in France learn how to use fire.

500,000 Early *Homo sapiens* in Europe use wooden spears with five hardened points, designed to pierce an animal's flesh.

1,000,000 — 750,000 — 500,000

A reconstruction of how early humans made stone tools.

Timeline

3.3 million years ago Evidence of the first stone tools

1.7 million years ago Hand axe technology, using one stone to shape another, comes into being

400,000 years ago Weapons dating from this time are the earliest spears to be found by archaeologists

60,000 years ago Date of the first arrowheads, found in southern Africa

They were made, not only made from rocks, but also from plants and bones. Most of the tools that have been discovered from this period by archaeologists are made of stone. Wooden tools have rotted away over the centuries.

The shapes and designs of tools depended on what they were being used for. When an animal was killed during hunting, sharp tools were necessary to skin it and cut up the meat. This had to be done quickly before larger predators arrived to take advantage of the kill. Stone was also chipped into small flakes that could be fitted onto a wooden shaft to make spears for use in hunting.

250,000 — 160,000 — 150,000 — 80,000

250,000 Early *Homo sapiens* in Africa, Asia, and Europe begin using stone axes.

c. 160,000 There is evidence that fire is used to prepare stone for making into tools.

150,000 European toolmakers insert a row of sharp flints into grooved pieces of wood or bone to make knives.

80,000 In Mesopotamia and Europe, people make stone lamps that burn oil or candle fat.

A digital illustration of Neanderthals hunting a bison using flint and wood spears. Neanderthals were a species of human that became extinct about 40,000 years ago.

Bows and arrows were likely introduced about 40,000 years ago. Although wooden bows from this period have not survived, archaeologists have found numerous arrowheads. Obsidian was particularly prized by Stone Age peoples. Like flint, obsidian can be split into sharp, wafer-thin shards, making it an ideal stone for arrowheads. Archaeologists have found obsidian artifacts all over the world, some far from their original source. This suggests that the highly-valued stone was traded by early humans.

TIMELINE

45,000 BCE –15,000 BCE

KEY:

Engineering and Technology

45,000 — 38,000 — 30,000

45,000 BCE People in Europe make stone-headed spears and flint knives.

38,000 BCE In Africa, people use a hook and line to catch fish.

30,000 Europeans use tally sticks, or notched pieces of bone, for counting.

Groups of early peoples living near rivers or the sea developed other tools. Freshwater fish and seafood were important foods. Early humans made fish hooks from bones or sea snail shells, and also caught fish using spears, harpoons, and nets. At the same time as they were making tools for hunting and protection, early human societies developed smaller tools for domestic purposes. Needles made from bone or antler were used to sew animal hides and fur together to make clothes. The "thread" was made from animal sinew or catgut, a type of cord made from animal intestines.

This is a modern reconstruction of a Stone Age axe. The shaped stone was attached to a wooden handle with ropes made from hemp or flax.

25,000 People in central Europe heat clay models to make ceramic images; they do not yet make clay pots.

20,000 In France, Cro-Magnon people produce stone blades shaped like leaves.

25,000

20,000

15,000

20,000 Europeans invent new hunting weapons, including the boomerang (made from mammoth tusk) and the wooden bow and arrow.

15,000 Africans use stone harpoons to spear fish.

Fire and Earth

Being able to control fire was a major advance in human development. It was used for warmth, cooking, and to make pottery vessels.

Natural wildfires spreading across forests, grasses, and grasslands would have been seen and feared by early humans millions of years ago. However, archaeologists have found evidence to suggest that the human species *Homo erectus* had begun to tame and use fire about 1.5 million years ago. Some scientists claim that the use of fire may have begun even earlier than that. How these early humans first came to control fire and keep it burning for their own uses is not known. But we do know that fire was an important step in the evolution of humans.

A forest fire rages. These fires were probably the first contact early humans had with fire.

TIMELINE

11,000 BCE –8500 BCE

KEY:

Life Sciences

Engineering and Technology

11,000 BCE Mediterranean people fish using nets.

11,000 Hunter-gatherers in northern Syria begin to cultivate rye.

11,000

11,000 BCE Clay pots are being made in Japan.

A man in Malaysia making fire by blowing onto a hot ember in dried grass.

Timeline

1 million years ago Evidence for the first use of fire by *Homo erectus*

400,000-300,000 years ago Fire is used for cooking food

164,000 years ago Evidence that stone is being heated to make it easier to work

29,000 years ago Clay figurines are made in central Europe

18,000 years ago Pottery vessels are being made from clay in Japan

Cooking Food

There is evidence, particularly from the Qesem cave in Israel, that fire was an essential part of human culture 400,000 years ago. The people who lived in the cave built hearths to contain fire and cook food. Some scientists believe it was cooking that led to important changes in humans. Because cooked food is softer than raw meat, teeth became smaller over time. The digestive tract also became shorter than that of other primates. It may even have been that the consumption of

10,000 People in Palestine make houses from sun-dried mud bricks, and weave baskets.

9000 In Palestine, farmers cultivate einkorn wheat; emmer wheat is grown in present-day Turkey.

10,000 | 9000 | 8500

10,000 Dogs are domesticated in Mesopotamia (modern Iraq), probably to keep as food but later as pets.

8500 Native peoples in North America make stone arrowheads.

A reconstruction of an early human settlement. The fire in the hearth is drying out animal bones and animal hides.

more calories from cooked meat and fish enabled the human brain to grow bigger and so become more effective at thinking and problem solving. And fire could also be used to preserve food, by smoking meat, for example.

By 100,000 years ago, humans were using fire to make tools. Wood was fire-hardened to make stronger spear points, while stones were heated to make it easier to chip them into hand axes. Sharp flakes were used as knives.

TIMELINE

8000 BCE –6300 BCE

KEY:

Life Sciences

Engineering and Technology

8000 BCE Goats and sheep are domesticated in East Africa and Mesopotamia.

8000

8000 BCE In Central America, people cultivate pumpkins and squashes.

7500

7500 The Mesopotamians use clay tokens for record keeping.

Making Pots

The effects of fire on clay (fine-grained soil) were also observed by modern humans, *Homo sapiens*. Clay becomes permanently hard when it is burned. By about 30,000 years ago, humans had begun making small ornaments by molding clay into a shape and then burning (firing) it to make it hard. While molding clay, some humans found that if they fired a clay bowl it would hold water.

The ability to carry water in pots meant that individuals did not have to visit a water source very day. One person could go and bring water back to the camp or village for everyone. Over thousands of years, pottery glazes were developed to make vessels more waterproof and decorative. Control of fire and water was essential to the development of the first civilizations.

Pottery from 2,000 years ago, made by people living along the Dnieper River. Pottery remains are one of the most accurate ways for archaeologists to identify different cultures.

7000 In Asia Minor (modern Turkey), pigs are domesticated for meat and leather.

6500 Cattle are domesticated in Africa and Asia.

7000

6500

6300

6500 The Chinese, who have gathered wild rice for centuries, cultivate rice in the Yangtze delta.

6300 Found in the Netherlands, the earliest dug-out boat was hollowed from a tree trunk about this time.

Invention of the Wheel

The wheel has been reinvented several times. It first appeared at least 5,000 years ago, but opinion is divided on how the original invention might have happened.

Inspiration for the vehicular wheel may have come from the potter's wheel.

TIMELINE

5000 BCE –4236 BCE

KEY:

Life Sciences

Engineering and Technology

5000 BCE People in Italy make the first mirrors, from obsidian.

5000 Egyptians smelt copper from its ore and use it to make weapons and other implements.

5000

5000 BCE In Mesopotamia, people use rod-shaped distaffs to spin yarn from wool.

5000 Arable farming begins in Mexico and Central America, where farmers grow corn (maize).

The wheel is one of the most adaptable inventions. It led to the development of cogs, gears, engine flywheels—and spinning wheels.

Timeline

3500 BCE The first potters' wheels appear in Mesopotamia

3200 BCE The first axled vehicular wheel appears (also in Mesopotamia)

2800 BCE The Chinese develop the wheel

2000 BCE The Sumerians develop the spoked wheel

85 BCE The waterwheel is developed in Greece

100 CE The Chinese invent the wheelbarrow

500–1000 CE The spinning wheel is developed in China

Six thousand years ago, humans were already using drag technology such as plows and sledges. In parts of the world, heavy objects such as rocks and boats were moved using log rollers. As the object moved forward, rollers were taken from behind and replaced in front.

Possible Evolution of the Wheel

At some point it seems likely that someone combined the use of a sledge with the rolling logs. Eventually the sledge would settle into the worn section of the rollers, and maybe this gave people the idea of the axle wheel.

But there are problems with the roller theory—logs split quite easily when rolled under pressure, and tall, straight trees were not abundant in the Middle East, where the first solid evidence for the making of transportation wheels appears.

4500 Central Americans cultivate avocados for food and cotton for yarn.

4400 Egyptians use linen made from wild flax to weave cloth on a loom.

4300 In France, people make oak canoes up to 16 feet (5 m) long.

4236 The ancient Egyptians introduce a 365-day calendar.

4500 | 4400 | 4300 | 4236

The Sumerians developed wheeled chariots, followed by the ancient Egyptians.

The Supernatural Wheel

There is no evidence that the wheel was used in ancient America. However, a hoard of what seem to be wheeled toys was carved in stone in Mexico in about 1500 BCE. So if the Aztecs knew how to make wheels, why didn't they use them? One theory is that the "toys" are, in fact, religious artifacts and that the wheel was seen as holy—it was reserved for the use of the Aztec gods alone.

Stone "toys" show that the Aztecs understood the idea of the wheel.

The development of a wheel that rotates on a fixed axle is used by archaeologists as an indicator of relatively advanced civilization. The earliest evidence of axled wheels dates back to about 3200 BCE. The Sumerian people of Mesopotamia (modern-day Iraq) produced pictures of carts with solid wheels, with axles through the center. Similar wheels appeared on war chariots built by the Sumerians in about 2500 BCE. About 500 years later, the Sumerians developed spoked wheels, which made chariots more maneuverable and lighter. Over the next 500 years, the design spread and was refined by other civilizations, including the Egyptians and the Romans.

The first wheels were probably not intended for transportation. Evidence from around 3500 BCE shows that potters were using simple turntables to help them create smooth pots. These early potters' wheels were developed further by the Greeks and

TIMELINE

4000 BCE –3500 BCE

KEY:

Life Sciences

Engineering and Technology

4000

4000 BCE The horse is domesticated in Ukraine, initially as food and later as a beast of burden.

4000 Potatoes are domesticated as a crop in the highlands of the Andes.

4000 BCE Builders in Egypt and Mesopotamia learn to construct arches.

4000 The first lock is invented in Mesopotamia.

Egyptians into flywheels that could convert pulses of energy, such as the pressing of a treadle, into smooth, continuous motion. The flywheel was to become just as important as the vehicular wheel. The Greeks also came up with other crucial mechanical variations on the wheel. The fourth and third centuries BCE saw the development of cogs, gearwheels, and pulleys. The waterwheel was another important variation. Developed around 85 BCE, waterwheels allowed humans to harness the power of water to drive heavy machinery, such as millstones.

Since ancient times there have been more wheel innovations. The Chinese began using spinning wheels for manufacturing yarn between 500 CE and 1000, for example. The spinning wheel is a variation on the flywheel: as the wheel turns, it rotates a spindle that twists fibers together to make thread.

The flywheel was crucial to the Industrial Revolution. When connected to pistons driven by a steam engine, it converted pulses of raw power into smooth movement that could be used to drive machines such as locomotives. Later still came wheel-based innovations such as turbines, gyroscopes, and castor wheels, all variations on an ancient technology still going strong today.

This ancient waterwheel still functions today, lifting water to supply neighboring fields.

4000 In what is now Turkistan, people begin growing grape vines to make wine.

4000 The ancient Egyptians use donkeys as beasts of burden.

4000

3500 Farmers in China and Mesopotamia use the first plows.

3500 The wheel is invented in Mesopotamia, originally as a potter's wheel.

3500

Writing and Numbers

Early writing took the form of symbols that signified exactly what they represented; they slowly acquired more abstract meanings, and eventually developed into writing.

Egyptian hieroglyphs began as representations of objects, but later could stand for sounds as well as objects.

TIMELINE

3400 BCE –3000 BCE

KEY:

Life Sciences

Engineering and Technology

3400 BCE The Sumerians of Mesopotamia use a simple form of picture writing.

3200 BCE Bronze, an alloy of copper and tin, is first used in Mesopotamia. It spreads through the Middle East and Europe.

3200 The Egyptians build nilometers to measure the height of the Nile and predict the annual flood.

3200 The first wheeled vehicles are used in western Asia.

3400

3200

Writing developed as a way of keeping records. It began with simple drawings: "sun" might be a circle inside a larger circle, and "water" might be depicted as a wavy line. In time, such signs came to have more than one meaning. The sign for "sun" also meant "day," or in Egypt the sun god Re (or Ra).

In the next stage each sign came to represent a sound as well as an object, or simply a sound. This type of writing, in which pictures represent sounds, is called "hieroglyphics." (Each picture is known as a "hieroglyph.") The best-known type was developed in Egypt, where it first appeared around 3100 BCE.

At about the same time another system of writing was emerging in Mesopotamia, in present-day Iraq. It also began as a system of stylized pictures, but it developed very differently from hieroglyphics, because of the tools used to write it. Egyptian scribes wrote on papyrus paper with pens and ink, but Mesopotamian scribes pressed a writing tool called a stylus into soft clay, making a wedge or round shape. This type of writing is called cuneiform. It came into use in about 2400 BCE, and was used by the Sumerians, Assyrians, and Babylonians. It also spread to Persia and remained in use for nearly 2,000 years.

Timeline

3400 BCE Numbers (base 10) used in Egypt

3100 BCE Egyptian hieroglyphs

2400 BCE Cuneiform writing

1700 BCE Early Chinese writing

1700 BCE Proto-Canaanite alphabet

1000 BCE Phoenician alphabet

Sumerian cuneiform was pressed into clay using a wedged-shaped stylus.

3100 Egyptians begin using hieroglyphs as a form of writing.

3000 The Mediterranean island of Cyprus becomes the ancient world's major source of copper.

3100

3000

3000 People settle in the Aegean region of Greece.

3000 The first pottery in the Americas is made in Ecuador and Colombia.

Babylonian Math Lives

The math we use today is to base 10, and the value of a digit depends on its position. So, 87 is 8 "tens" plus 7 "units." The Babylonians used base 60. They would have written 87 as 1 "sixty" plus 27, or 1 27. It is similar to the way we might write 87 minutes as 1 hour 27 minutes. This is no coincidence. We still use the Babylonian base 60 system for time (hours, minutes, and seconds) and for geometry (degrees, minutes, and seconds). There are 360 degrees (six "sixties") in a circle.

The first real alphabet (the Proto Canaanite) emerged in the Middle East in about 1700 BCE. It used 30 symbols to represent single sounds. From this, the Phoenician alphabet of 22 letters developed by about 1000 BCE, later giving rise to Arabic, Hebrew, Latin, and Greek scripts.

Chinese writing also developed from pictures. The symbols were in use from about 1700 BCE. They became more abstract during the Zhou Dynasty (c.1122–256 BCE).

Hieroglyphs were slow to write, so Egyptians then developed an easier, quicker script.

Counting Numbers

Record keepers also needed a way to write numbers. A picture of one cow can represent one cow, but it would be impractical to show 60 cows by drawing each one. In about 30,000 BCE in what is now the Czech Republic, someone carved 11 groups of five notches on a bone. It is clearly a numerical record. A stick or bone used in this way is called a tally stick.

Numerals greater than 10 were first used in Egypt in about 3400 BCE and

TIMELINE

2900 BCE –2600 BCE

KEY:

Life Sciences

Engineering and Technology

2900 BCE People in the Indus Valley in India cultivate cotton and spin its fibers into yarn.

2800 The Egyptians use fibers from reeds to make papyrus, an early form of paper.

2900

2800

2800 The Sumerians make soap from animal fat and plant ashes.

Roman letters often had straight lines so they were easy to carve in stone.

in Mesopotamia in about 3000 BCE. Most cultures used 10 as a base, probably because humans have 10 fingers. The Babylonians and Sumerians were exceptions; they calculated to base 60.

Egyptian and cuneiform numbers used different symbols for 1; 10; 100; 1,000; 10,000; 100,000; and 1,000,000, and indicated higher values by repeating them, as in Roman numerals, where X is 10, XX is 20, and XXX is 30; C is 100, and CCC is 300. However, none of these systems had a zero.

Thousands of cuneiform tablets have survived. Some were used by students to learn multiplication tables and complex calculations. Egyptians, on the other hand, used only addition and the two times table. They multiplied by repeatedly doubling or halving and then adding the results.

Most of the letters in our modern English alphabet can be traced back to the Phoenician alphabet, as shown here. However, the Phoenicians made no distinction between the letter J and the letter I.

2750 Mesopotamian builders use corbeled arches to build arches and domes.

2700 In China, silkworms are raised on mulberry leaves; their cocoons are unwound to make silk.

2630 Work begins on the step pyramid of King Djoser, the first pyramid in Egypt.

2600 People in Mesopotamia make glass by melting silica (sand) and soda.

2750 | 2700 | 2630 | 2600

Agriculture and Food

About 11,000 years ago, people began to give up the hunter-gatherer way of life and live in settlements where they could grow crops and rear animals.

This Egyptian tomb painting shows a farmer using an ox to pull a plow.

TIMELINE

2550 BCE –2300 BCE

KEY:

Life Sciences

Engineering and Technology

Astronomy and Math

2550 BCE The Great Pyramid of King Khufu (Cheops) is completed at Giza in Egypt.

2500 Clay water pipes are used at Knossos in Crete and Mohenjo-Daro in what is now Pakistan.

2550

2500

2500 BCE In Egypt, physicians begin to practice surgery and develop medical instruments.

2500 Sumerian traders introduce a standard system of weights and measures.

In some regions of the world, fields are still tilled as they were in ancient times, by oxen pulling simple wooden plows.

In the fertile valley of the Nile River in Egypt and in Mesopotamia between the Tigris and Euphrates Rivers (in present-day Iraq), early farmers used digging sticks and hoes to prepare the soil for planting and sickles to harvest crops. The plow, invented in about 3500 BCE in Mesopotamia and China, greatly extended the areas of land that could be tilled to grow food. Over the years, selective breeding resulted in higher-yielding strains of cereal plants such as wheat and barley. People also applied domestication and selective

Different types of wheat were domesticated over about 3000 years.

2400 The Egyptians domesticate cats; they see some cats as sacred and make them into mummies.

2400 Mesopotamians invent the umbrella or parasol.

2300 Babylonian astronomers study constellations and other heavenly phenomena.

2300 Work begins on stone circles at Stonehenge in England, already an ancient ceremonial center.

2400

2300

Crops in the New World

Cereal crops were the first to be cultivated. Barley and wheat were probably first, then rice and corn (maize). Next, between 8,000 and 5,000 years ago, came root crops and legumes, such as beets and beans. Later still were fruiting trees, leafy vegetables, and crops grown to feed livestock. By 2,000 years ago, crops such as medicinal and cooking herbs were under cultivation. Some plants even began to be grown for their decorative value.

breeding to animals. Beasts of burden, such as horses, oxen, and buffalo, began to replace human muscle power to carry loads, draw plows, and pull carts.

Storing and Processing Food

It was difficult to keep food over the winter, although people did store dried grain. Pulses (edible seeds), such as lentils and beans, could also be dried. Farmers killed many of their animals in late fall because they had insufficient food for them over the winter. People preserved animal carcasses simply by

Farming was painted in Egyptian tombs to ensure that the dead person had enough to eat in the afterlife.

TIMELINE

2200 BCE –2000 BCE

KEY:

Life Sciences

Engineering and Technology

2200 BCE Iron is used for weapons in what is now Turkey.

2100 BCE The Sumerians build a ziggurat (temple) of sun-dried mud bricks at Ur.

2050 Large cities are built in the Indus valley. About 40,000 people live in the city of Harappa.

allowing them to dry in the wind, and in cold climates stored them in caves. New technologies arose from the need to store and preserve food. One method involved smoking meat or fish over a fire, a method still used today. Fish and meat were also salted. Curing (smoking) and salting of pig meat (pork) created ham and bacon.

Using Grindstones

People also began to use grindstones to make flour from harvested grains and to make clay pots to store food as well as for cooking. The earliest known pottery dates from about 11,000 BCE in Japan. It was invented independently in the Middle East about 5,000 years later. As the potters grew more skillful, they built ovens for baking the clay.

An 18th-century print shows harvesting with sickles, first used in ancient Egypt.

2000 People in Peru domesticate guinea pigs for food.

2000 Chinese emperors keep animals in one of the first zoos, called the Park of Intelligence.

2000

2000 Austronesians use outrigger boats to explore and populate the Pacific Islands.

2000 In Syria and Babylon, doctors practice medicine based on astrology.

Ancient Medicine

Throughout history, doctors have healed the sick. In the ancient world, however, medical understanding of how the body worked was relatively limited.

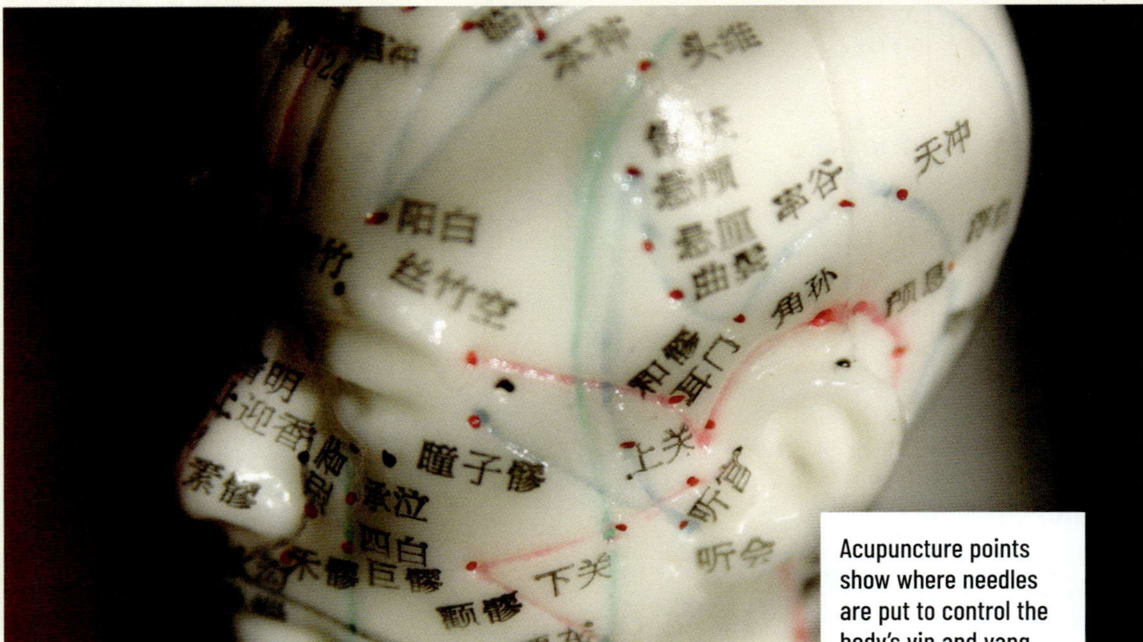

Acupuncture points show where needles are put to control the body's yin and yang.

TIMELINE

2000 BCE –1600 BCE

KEY:

- Life Sciences
- Engineering and Technology
- Astronomy and Math

2000 | 1950 | 1900

2000 BCE Spoked wheels are used on chariots in Egypt and the Middle East.

1950 BCE In Palestine, farmers make plows with iron blades.

1900 In Persia (now Iran), farmers cultivate alfalfa as a fodder crop for animals.

A Chinese symbol shows a perfect balance between yin and yang.

People who had not yet learned how the human body functions believed there were two classes of illness. Trivial complaints, such as an upset stomach, headache, or cold, were part of everyday life. People put up with them and treated them with whatever remedy seemed to work.

More serious illnesses, such as fevers or dysentery, were the work of demons or of gods who had been offended. They avenged themselves by throwing darts or worms into the victim's body or by extracting some important part—often the soul. Treatment involved removing the dart, worm, or demon causing the symptoms or encouraging the soul to return to its proper place. Practitioners would use suction or manipulation of the patient's body as well as administer herbal

Timeline

2500 BCE Imhotep is the Egyptian god of medicine

2500 BCE Acupuncture is practiced in China

1790 BCE Hammurabi, king of Babylon, lays down laws to punish doctors for mistakes

1200 BCE Asclepius, the Greek god of medicine, may have flourished around this time

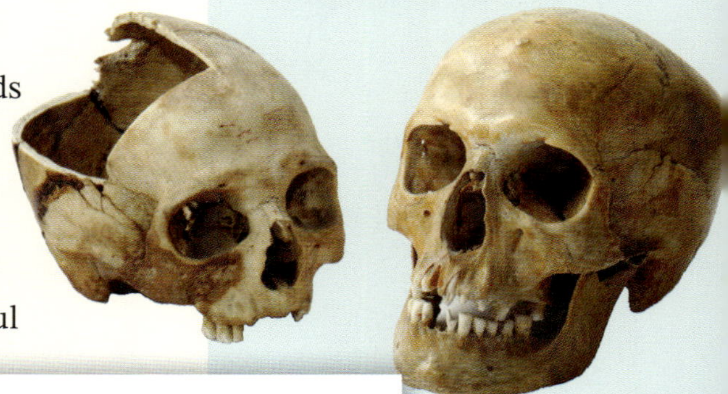

Some ancient skulls have holes made in them, probably to release the evil spirits believed to cause mental illnesses.

1800 Mathematicians in Mesopotamia discover what is now known as the Pythagorean Theorem.

1750 In Babylon, King Hammurabi asks astronomers to compile catalogs of stars and planets.

1700 People in Syria develop a phonetic alphabet with 30 symbols, each representing a sound.

1600 Astrologers in Babylon recognize the zodiac, the path of the sun, moon, and planets through the sky.

1600 Bellows are used in Mediterranean countries to increase the heat of fires for metalworking and glassworking.

1800 1750 1700 1600

medicines and perform incantations. Treatment therefore involved magic or religious ritual, and those who performed it were known as "medicine men" or "medicine women."

Drilling a hole 1 to 2 inches (2.5 to 5 cm) across in the top of the skull was one way to allow whatever caused an illness to escape. This was called trepanning, and it was practiced in many parts of the world. Prehistoric trepanned skulls have been found in Europe and also in Peru. The patient often survived the treatment. In the ancient skulls, bone has regrown to seal the holes.

Greek God of Healing

In Greek mythology, Asclepius was raised by a centaur who taught him healing, and the Greeks worshipped him as the god of healing. Hundreds of temples to Asclepius were built across Greece. Sick people slept at the temples and were visited by Asclepius in a dream. The next day they told their dreams to priests, who gave them advice about what was needed to cure them.

Ayurvedic yoga is still practiced today, as a healthy exercise and also as part of Hinduism.

China and India

Chinese medicine began over 4,500 years ago. Chinese doctors believed that illness was caused by imbalances between the female (yin) and male (yang) cosmic principles, and their treatment aimed to correct the imbalance. Doctors used herbal remedies, including ginseng.

TIMELINE

1550 BCE –1500 BCE

KEY:

Life Sciences

Engineering and Technology

1550 BCE An Egyptian papyrus gives details of 700 drugs in use by Egyptian doctors.

1500 BCE On Crete, the Palace of Minos has bathrooms with running water.

1500 In Mexico, people make toys with wheels—but do not yet use wheels for transportation.

1500 On the Gulf Coast of Central America, the Olmec culture builds complexes of pyramids and temples.

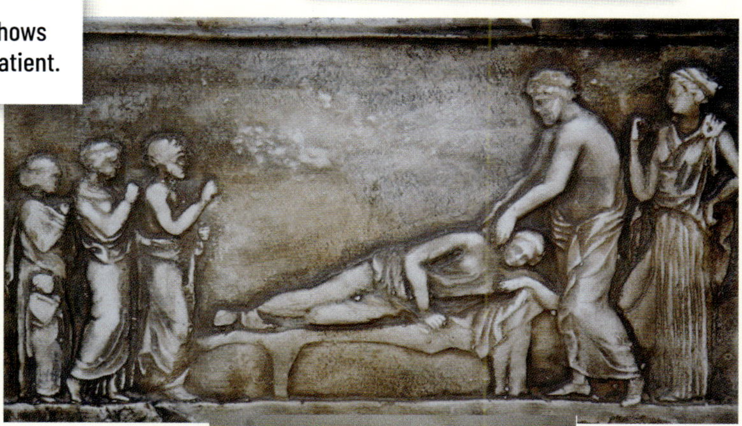

This Greek carving shows a doctor treating a patient.

Acupuncture was first practiced more than 4,500 years ago. Chinese scientists believed the body contained three "burning spaces" and that the cosmic principles (yin and yang) circulate through 12 channels. Acupuncture aims to alter the distribution of yin and yang in the channels and burning spaces. The technique involves inserting warm or cold metal needles into the skin at particular points on the body that are related to particular organs. There are hundreds of such points.

Ayurvedic medicine, based on religious writings called the "Vedas," is still used in India, where it began about 3,000 years ago. The aim is to prevent illness through lifestyle, hygiene, and yoga, and to cure complaints by using herbal and mineral preparations and the correct diet. Ayurvedic practitioners treat the whole person rather than simply dealing with a particular illness.

The Greek physician Hippocrates of Cos, after whom the doctors' Hippocratic oath is named, is seen as the father of medicine.

1500 People in China make beer from cereals.

1500 The Egyptians use the shaduf—a bucket on a long lever—to raise water from rivers for irrigation.

1500

1500 The Mitani of what is now Armenia learn to smelt iron from its ore; the technique passes to the Hittites.

The Pyramids

The Great Pyramid at Giza is still standing after 4,500 years. That demonstrates the technological skill and ingenuity of the ancient civilization that built it.

The Great Pyramid rises behind the Sphinx, a statue of a lion with a man's head.

TIMELINE

1450 BCE –1100 BCE

KEY:

Engineering and Technology

Astronomy and Math

1450 1400 1361

1450 BCE The Egyptians use a water clock (clepsydra) to tell the time.

1400 BCE Stonehenge is completed in southern England.

1361 Chinese astronomers record the first known solar eclipse.

Humankind seems compelled to create tall buildings. Four thousand years ago, the only shape for such a structure was a broad base tapering at the top. Smooth-sided pyramids seem to have been a progression from the ziggurats built in Mesopotamia and Persia between 3000 and 500 BCE. A ziggurat was a temple-tower built in several levels, each smaller than the one below. It may have represented a sacred mountain or a link between Earth and heaven. Ziggurats had from two to seven tiers built of mud.

Pyramids in Egypt

The first pyramid in Egypt was built at Saqqara in about 2630 BCE. It had a stepped structure, but was made of stone rather than mud. Within 30 years, the Egyptians had refined the design and were building smooth pyramids, such as the Red Pyramid at Dahshur, seen as the first "true" pyramid. The massive blocks at the core were cased in smaller blocks to smooth the outline.

The pyramids were burial structures built to honor the kings (or pharaohs), who were seen as living gods. Detailed plans were drawn up by skilled draftsmen working on sheets of papyrus.

Timeline

2630 BCE First pyramid built in Egypt at Saqqara

2600 BCE First true pyramid, the Red Pyramid at Dahshur, is built

2550 BCE Great Pyramid at Giza completed

2250 BCE Last pyramid built in Egypt, for Pharaoh Pepi II at Saqqara

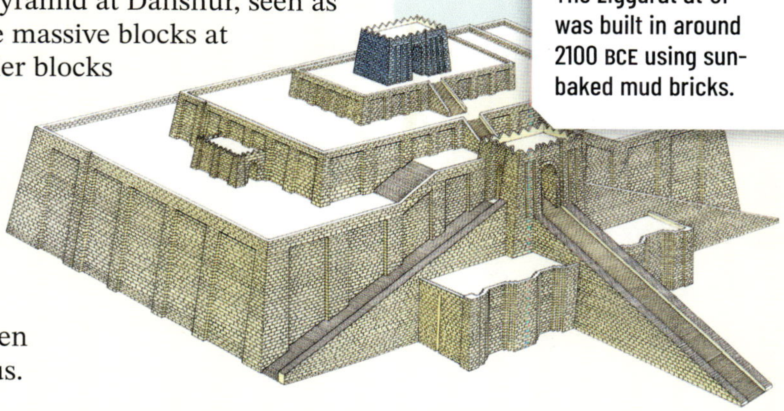

The ziggurat at Ur was built in around 2100 BCE using sun-baked mud bricks.

1350 Egyptians and Hittites begin working with iron.

1200 Coastal fishermen in Peru make rafts and boats from reeds.

1150 Chinese workers cast bells from bronze.

1100 In China, craftsmen use spinning to produce yarn from cotton and wool.

1350 1200 1150 1100

Which Ramps?

The ramps used by the pyramid builders are the subject of much speculation. The simplest ramps approached one side of the pyramid. But to maintain a shallow gradient, they would have to have been very long and contain almost as much building material as the pyramid itself. Other ramp designs, such as zigzags and spirals, would have used less material but would be more complex structurally.

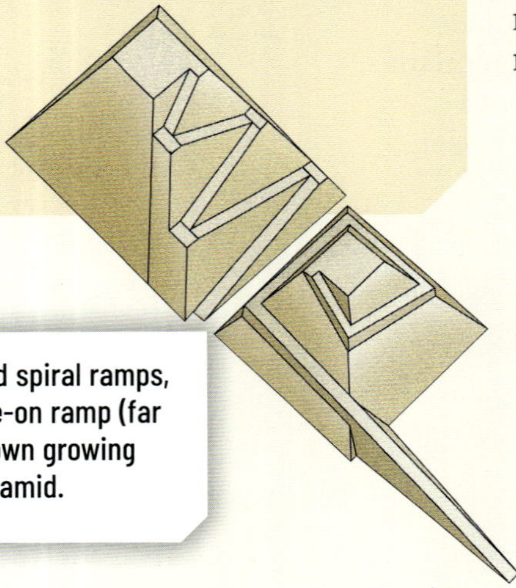

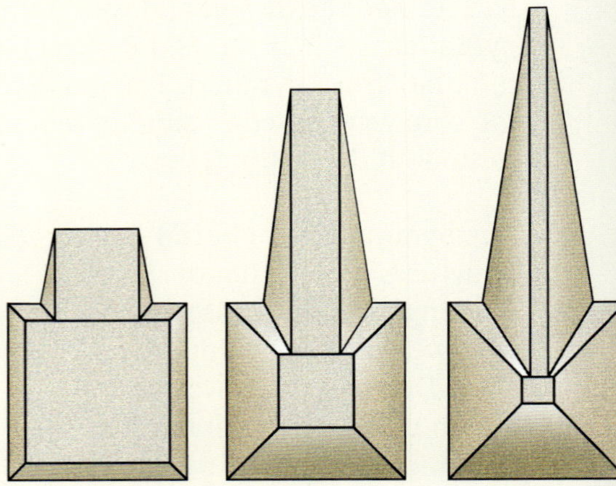

Zigzag and spiral ramps, and a side-on ramp (far right), shown growing with a pyramid.

Sometimes the pyramids were built over natural features such as rocky outcrops. This meant that fewer materials had to be imported but made surveying and measuring more difficult.

Engineering the Pyramids

Egyptian pyramids are built along a precise north–south axis. The Egyptians used a surveying tool called a bay to determine true north from the stars. The pyramids show that the Egyptians also knew geometry. Anything less than a perfect square at the base would mean that the four sides would fail to form a neat point at the apex at the top. The same

TIMELINE

1050 BCE –980 BCE

KEY:

Life Sciences

Engineering and Technology

Astronomy and Math

1050 BCE Invaders from Anatolia introduce ironworking to Greece.

1050

1000 Chinese scribes write on bamboo or tree bark using brushes and black ink made from ashes and tree gum.

1000

1000 BCE The kite is invented in China; it is probably the first heavier-than-air flying object.

This diagram shows the complex structure of a pyramid, with chambers, access tunnels, and air vents.

Moving the Blocks

The stone blocks for the pyramids weighed many tons. They were quarried as nearby as possible or brought by boat along the Nile River. To carry the stone to the top of the pyramid, the builders used huge straight or zigzag ramps up which they could drag the blocks on wooden sleds. At the top, levers were used to maneuver the blocks into position.

perfection was required of the stone blocks, which were shaped by skilled masons. The real secret of the pyramids may lie in the use of a vast workforce. Estimates of the numbers involved vary from 100,000 to just a few thousand. It is unlikely that these people were slaves. There is archaeological evidence of communities centered on the construction sites, providing housing and services for a huge, highly specialized workforce.

The pyramids were made from huge blocks of stone with an outer casing of smaller blocks.

1000 The Phoenicians of the eastern Mediterranean introduce a 22-letter alphabet.

980 A Chinese writer recommends using steam to sterilize objects.

1000

980

1000 A calendar of 12 lunar months is used in India.

1000 In Italy, Etruscan craftsmen use gold to make false teeth.

Using Metals

Egyptians were making copper tools and weapons around 7,000 years ago. As the technology spread, new, improved metals shaped the development of society.

The so-called Mask of Agamemnon was made from gold in c.1500 BCE.

TIMELINE

950 BCE–850 BCE

KEY:

Life Sciences

Engineering and Technology

950 BCE Farmers in northern and central Europe grow oats, which are better suited to the cool climate than wheat.

925 Etruscans are mining tin and copper in central Italy.

950

925

950 BCE The Phoenicians make purple dye from the Murex sea mollusk; it is so rare and expensive that only rulers are allowed to wear clothes dyed with it.

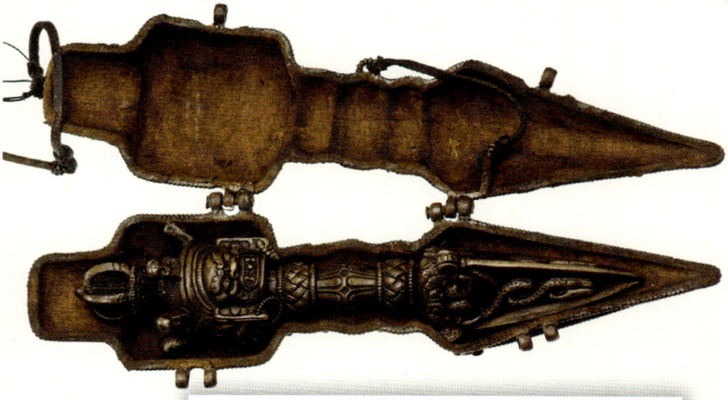

Ancient daggers were often used as ritual objects rather than for practical purposes.

Some of the earliest metal artifacts are of gold and silver. In Egypt, the famous burial mask of Tutankhamun was made from gold. Gold and silver vessels, ceremonial weapons, and ornaments have been found in graves throughout the eastern Mediterranean and western Asia. However, on its own or alloyed with silver to make electrum, gold is too soft for making tools or weapons. Gold and silver were purely decorative.

The Copper Age

Copper was different. In order to use copper, the lumps of metal must be melted and then cast in molds. Hammering then hardens the copper, allowing it to be

Timeline

c.5000 BCE Egyptian weapons and tools made of copper

c.3200 BCE Bronze produced throughout the Middle East

c.3000 BCE Copper axes produced in the Balkans in southeastern Europe

c.2000 BCE Iron produced by metalworkers in southern India

c.1600 BCE Mycenaean daggers with bronze, gold, and silver

c.1400 BCE Ironworking becomes important to the Hittites of Anatolia (Turkey)

1323 BCE Egyptian king Tutankhamun is buried with a funeral mask made of gold inlaid with lapis lazuli

c.1000 BCE Ironworking has spread across Europe

900 In Mesopotamia, farmers use irrigation to get better harvests.

850 The first known stone arch bridge is built at Smyrna, now Izmir in Turkey.

900

850

900 The Chinese cast metal coins in the shape of shovels or knives.

850 The Chinese use natural gas—probably methane from underground deposits—for lighting, conveyed along "pipes" of bamboo.

Rich Egyptians were buried with lavish jewelry made from precious metals.

used to make blades. Weapons and tools were made from copper in Egypt by 5000 BCE, and copper axes were being made in the Balkans by 3000 BCE. People also discovered that they produced more copper if they melted it in the presence of a particular blue stone. They had begun to extract a metal from its ore, in this case azurite.

The Bronze Age

Sometime after 4000 BCE, people began to mix tin with copper to form the alloy bronze. It is much harder than copper, and bronze tools stay sharper longer. Bronze was made in what is now southern Iraq between 3200 and 2500 BCE. It spread relatively quickly throughout the Middle East and Europe. As it did so, the Copper Age gave way to the Bronze Age.

The Coming of Iron

Iron is difficult to obtain from its ore because it has a very high melting point; the process also needs repeated melting and hammering. But iron was being

TIMELINE

800 BCE–600 BCE

KEY:

- Life Sciences
- Engineering and Technology
- Astronomy and Math

800 — **800 BCE** Egyptians use artificially heated incubators to hatch eggs.

763 — **763 BCE** Babylonian astronomers record an eclipse of the sun.

750 — **750** The Greek poet Homer records the burning of sulfur to fumigate plants and kill pests.

produced in southern India around 2000 BCE. An iron dagger blade dating from about 2200 BCE was found in Anatolia (now Turkey). Iron was important to the Hittites by 1400 BCE and by 1000 BCE had spread across Europe.

Iron is soft, so it could not compete with bronze. But smiths found that iron is strengthened if it is kept at bright-red heat in a charcoal fire. By absorbing carbon from the charcoal, iron is converted into steel, which is made stronger still if it is plunged into water while red hot. Steel was first made in India in about the third century BCE. Stories about swords with special powers probably refer to steel blades that were stronger than bronze.

Alloys

An alloy is a mixture of two or more metals, often with small amounts of other elements. Alloys are made by isolating the metallic ingredients, mixing the metals in the required proportions, and finally melting the metals together. The properties of an alloy differ from those of the metals that make it. The first alloys were of copper and tin, which make bronze. The finest bronze contains 89 percent copper and 10 percent tin, with very small amounts of other added metals.

A bronze helmet worn by a Greek soldier, with openings only for the eyes and mouth.

700 Phoenicians build biremes—boats with two rows of oars on either side.

691 King Sennacherib of Assyria builds a 50-mile (80 km) aqueduct to carry water to his capital, Nineveh.

600 In Central America, the Maya use pods from the cacao plant to make drinking chocolate.

600 The Greek artist Glaucus of Chios produces an alloy that melts easily and uses it to solder metals.

Calendars

Around 35,000 years ago, Africans carved notches on bones to mark the passage of time. Similar "calendar sticks" were made until relatively recently by Native Americans.

A carved Aztec calendar, showing periods of time around the image of a god.

TIMELINE

560 BCE–430 BCE

KEY:

Life Sciences

Engineering and Technology

Astronomy and Math

560 BCE The Greek philosopher Xenophanes of Colophon realizes that the presence of fossil seashells high on mountains means that the land was once below sea level.

550 BCE The Greek mathematician Pythagoras works out the relationship between the length of a vibrating string and the note it produces.

535 The Greek physician Alcmaeon dissects animals to study their anatomy.

560 550 535

The Egyptian calendar was developed to predict the annual Nile River flood.

Another African calendar, the Ishango bone, dates from 25,000 years ago. It probably counts the days from new moon to new moon (lunar cycle), over a period of six months.

All early calendars were based on this lunar cycle, including the first annual calendar, developed by the Egyptians in about 4236 BCE. However, the lunar calendar failed to predict the seasonal flooding of the Nile River. Egyptian astronomers found that when the star Sirius was visible shortly before sunrise, the Nile flood followed a few days later. They devised a calendar based on a solar year and lunar months. It had three seasons, each of four months of 30 days, with an extra five days at

Timeline

33,000 BCE Lebombo bone carved in what is now Swaziland

23,000 BCE Ishango bone carved in present-day Democractic Republic of Congo

423 BCE The full Egyptian lunar calendar is made

3000 BCE Sumerian calendar of months of 30 days

2950 BCE The Chinese lunar calendar

1800 BCE The Sumerian lunar-year calendar

1700 BCE Babylon adopts the Sumerian calendar from Nippur

1100 BCE The Assyrians adopt the Babylonian calendar

1000 BCE Hindu lunar calendar

515

515 The philosopher Anaximander of Miletus introduces the sundial to Greece as a way of telling the time.

513

513 King Darius of Persia builds a 2000-foot (610-m) floating bridge to allow his army to cross the Bosphorus to invade Greece.

434

434 Anaxagoras of Iona suggests that the sun is a ball of hot rock.

430

430 In four famous paradoxes, Zeno of Elea challenges the accepted ideas about time and space.

Early astronomers based the first calendars on the regular movements of stars and other heavenly bodies.

the end of the year, making a year of 365 days. They also used a measurement of time longer than a year: the reign of a king.

It was the Egyptians who first divided the day into 24 units. The units were not of equal length, however. There were 12 daytime units and 12 nighttime units, and their lengths changed with the seasons.

The Sumerian Calendar

By about 3000 BCE, the Sumerians of what is now southern Iraq had divided the year into 12 months of 30 days each. There were 12 periods in a day, each divided into 30 parts. The Sumerians also invented other calendars. The year began at the time of the barley harvest, but the financial year began about two months later, when the grain was sent to market. The commencement of the year was a time when the king made offerings to the gods. The Sumerian calendar was adopted by the Babylonians in the 18th century BCE and, later, by the Assyrians.

The zodiac was developed by the Babylonians, based on the movement of stars.

TIMELINE

424 BCE–350 BCE

KEY:

- Life Sciences
- Engineering and Technology
- Astronomy and Math

424

424 BCE In wars between city-states in Greece, attackers use flamethrowers made of tubes holding burning charcoal, sulfur, and tar.

400

400 The Chinese use counting boards with bamboo rods to make calculations.

400 BCE Hippocrates of Kos, said to be the founder of the Hippocratic oath taken by doctors today, describes human anatomy and the causes of some diseases.

400 Mayan mathematicians develop a number system using base 20.

From about 2950 BCE, the Chinese developed a lunar calendar. It divides the year into 12 months of alternately 29 and 30 days, with additional months added from time to time to keep the calendar in step with the solar year.

The Hindu calendar, introduced around 1000 BCE, divides the year into 12 lunar months of 27 or 28 days, with an additional month inserted every five years. The year is also divided into three periods of four months. The start of each period is marked by a religious festival.

Months and Days

Sometime before 2100 BCE, Sumerians began using lunar years. This meant that a loan made in a certain month could be repaid in the same month the following year. In about 1800 BCE, this produced a calendar of 12 months alternating between 29 and 30 days. The resulting year of 354 days (29 x 6) + (30 x 6) failed to coincide with the agricultural year as measured by the sun. So for this reason, Sumerian cities inserted an extra month. The insertion was not standardized, so each city had its own calendar.

This observatory was used by ancient Indian astronomers to study the heavens.

399 Authorities in Syracuse order the development of new weapons, including a repeating arrow-firing catapult.

387 The Greek thinker Plato opens an academy in Athens for the pursuit of philosophy and scientific research.

350 Aristotle draws up a classification scheme for animals and plants.

399 → 387 → 350

Boats and Ships

The use of vessels to cross the oceans was crucial to the development of humankind. Building, sailing, and maintaining boats were great technological achievements of the ancient world.

By about 40,000 years ago, people from southeast Asia had crossed the seas to Australia. They must have done this in boats, but there are no records of what these craft looked like or how they were powered. The earliest known depiction of a boat dates from about 10,000 years ago. It is a rock carving that was found in Norway, which suggests that Stone Age Scandinavians were using vessels. To make boats, early humans must have used materials that float. The first boats in Mesopotamia were small vessels made from bundles of papyrus reeds lashed together with ropes. The reeds were covered with bitumen to make the vessel watertight. These boats were powered by oars and poles, and later by large, central sails.

A ceremonial boat of the type that would have been used on the Nile from about 1800 BCE. The hull is made from wood rather than papyrus reeds.

TIMELINE

340 BCE–214 BCE

KEY:

- Life Sciences
- Engineering and Technology
- Astronomy and Math

340 BCE The Greek physician Praxagoras of Kos distinguishes between veins and arteries.

330 BCE Greek philosopher Aristotle proposes that Earth is at the center of the universe and the planets, moon, sun, and stars orbit it.

312 Romans build the Aqua Appia, the first aqueduct to bring water into Rome.

340 330 312

Outrigger Vessels

The most efficient ships and boats built in the ancient world were those of the Austronesians. These people used single or double-hulled catamarans (small, narrow boats with outriggers projecting from the hull to provide stability). Catamarans were propelled by triangular sails. Austronesians travelled across the oceans, populating many of the Pacific islands. They set out from what is now Taiwan in about 2200 BCE, and reached Hawaii in about 1250 BCE. These types of catamarans greatly influenced Chinese shipbuilding.

In the Mediterranean, the ancient Egyptians used boats with oars and sails to transport goods along the River Nile. Warships were introduced in about 600 BCE. These ships were powered by banks of rowers.

Timeline

50,000 years ago Humans cross the sea to Australia

10,000 years ago Norwegian rock carving of a boat

2200 years ago Austronesians explore the Pacific islands

3500 BCE Reed boats used in the Persian Gulf

480 BCE Greek triremes defeat Persian vessels at the battle of Salamis

A Greek trireme, a slim, light warship that used its ram at the bow to attack and sink enemy vessels.

300 Greek mathematician Euclid writes *Elements*, a book of geometrical theorems.

283 Greek engineers build the Pharos lighthouse at Alexandria, Egypt; it is one of the Seven Wonders of the Ancient World.

235 In Greece, Eratosthenes calculates the circumference of Earth.

214 The main part of the Great Wall of China—some 1400 miles (2,250 km) long—is completed.

300 283 235 214

The arrangement of rowers on a trireme. The outrigger kept the top level of oars clear of those on the lower levels.

Warships

Most Mediterranean ships used both sails and oars. However, the sails were large and square, and were only effective if the wind was coming from the right direction. For warships, which needed to maneuver quickly at all times, the main propulsion was oars.

Triremes

One of the best known ancient warships was the Greek trireme. Triremes were light and about 120 ft (37 m) long. When there was not enough wind to use the sails, the boat was powered by three banks of oarsmen. The highest bank of oars rested on an outrigger. The lowest bank of oars was near the waterline. Leather covers around the oar holes stopped too much water entering the ship. On deck, triremes carried a small group of regular crew and soldiers (about 30 men), and projectile weapons such as catapults. However, the main weapon was an iron projection at the bow, which was used to ram enemy vessels.

TIMELINE

200 BCE–125 BCE

KEY:

Life Sciences

Engineering and Technology

Astronomy and Math

200 BCE In South America, metalworkers use blowpipes to create the draft for furnaces to make alloys of gold and silver.

200

200 BCE In what is now Peru, the Nazca begin "drawing" huge outlines of plants and animals in the desert.

165 Chinese astronomers record the existence of sunspots.

165

The wood for the hull and oars was carefully selected. It was largely cedar, pine, or fir, with oak on the outer hull. The use of soft woods made the trireme light and maneuverable, but it could become waterlogged. The ropes for the sails also had to be strong and able to withstand sea salt. Triremes did not sail at night, so ships were lifted out of the water and onto land.

The great age of the trireme was the period 500 to 300 BCE. After this, the Roman Empire gradually came to dominate the Mediterranean. The Romans used larger vessels, with four or five banks of oars, and with more weapons mounted on the decks. Their merchant vessels were usually propelled by sail, and operated seasonally, using the prevailing winds to cross the Mediterranean.

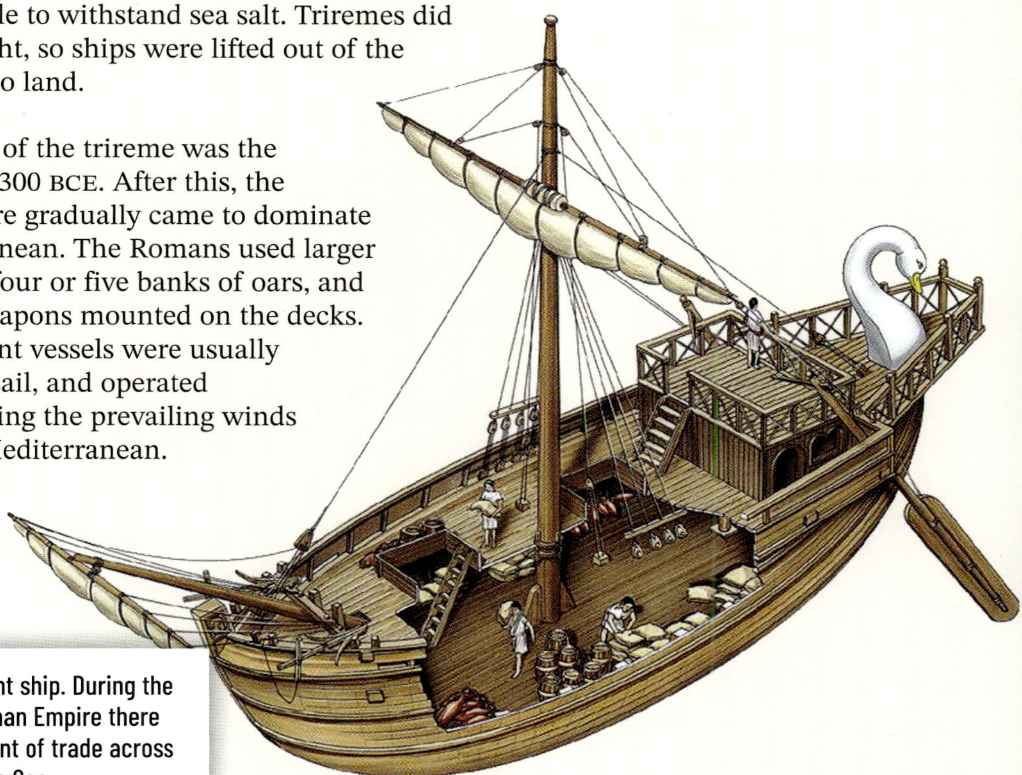

A Roman merchant ship. During the period of the Roman Empire there was a huge amount of trade across the Mediterranean Sea.

150 Greeks and Romans use a screw press to crush olives to extract olive oil.

125 Chinese traveler Chang Ch'ien introduces wine grapes into China from the West.

150

125

150 The Greek astronomer Hipparchus of Nicaea calculates the distance from Earth to the moon.

150 People in Ireland and Germany make roads by laying wooden planks together.

Aristotle

Few individuals have influenced so many different areas of learning as Aristotle. He informed generations in areas such as logic, meteorology, physics, and theology.

The School of Athens, painted in 1510, shows Aristotle and other ancient thinkers.

TIMELINE

110 BCE–46 BCE

KEY:

- Life Sciences
- Engineering and Technology
- Astronomy and Math

110 BCE Roman horsemen begin to use nailed horseshoes.

100 Chinese mathematicians begin to use negative numbers.

110

100

100 BCE Roman builders begin to use concrete made from crushed stones.

100 The Romans develop a system for heating seawater to cultivate oysters.

A bust of Aristotle is a familiar sight in many museums and places of learning in the West.

Timeline

384 BCE Aristotle born at Stagirus

367 BCE Studies at Plato's Academy in Athens

347 BCE Leaves Athens

342 BCE Becomes tutor to Alexander

336 BCE Alexander becomes king; Aristotle returns to Athens

335 BCE Aristotle founds the Lyceum

323 BCE Alexander dies; Aristotle retreats to Chalcis

322 BCE Aristotle dies

Possibly the most influential thinker ever to have lived, Aristotle was born in 384 BCE at Stagirus, a port in Macedonia. His studies took him to Athens to the Academy of the philosopher Plato (c.428–c.348 BCE). He then spent several years traveling in Asia Minor and studying natural history.

In 342 BCE, the new king of Macedon, Philip, asked Aristotle to be a tutor to his 14-year-old son Alexander—

Liber
Aristotelis Meteorologicorum Liber Primus/Interprete, et expositore Augustino Nipho Medice/Pho Suessano.

E primis quidem igitur causis naturę: et de omni motu naturali: adhuc autem de sm superiorē lationem preordinatis astris, et de elemētis corporeis, et quot, et qualia sint, et de ea/quę est inuicem permutatione: et de generatione, et corruptione cōmuni dictum est prius.

Retermissis bis, quę in librorum pcinijs expositores facere solent, Dicamus cū Alexādro aphrodisio Aristotelem pmo pmittere intētionem eorum, quę in hoc libro facturus est. Secūdo pcedere ad ppositę intētionis pertractationem. In pmittenda vero intentione eorum/quę in hoc libro est facturus/ad memoriā

A page from a 16th-century book on Aristotle. His work was read for centuries after his death.

80 Vertical waterwheels are used to grind corn in eastern Mediterranean regions.

75 The Greek physician Asclepiades of Bithynia asserts that disease is caused by discord in the body.

55 In India, the Hindu medical system called the Ayurveda becomes the basis of medical teaching.

52 A Chinese astronomer makes an armillary ring (used to represent the equator when observing stars).

46 Emperor Julius Caesar introduces the Julian calendar.

Aristotle's Astronomy

Aristotle showed that Earth is round by observing that during a lunar eclipse, Earth casts a shadow with a curved edge onto the moon. He also observed that, while traveling north or south, new stars appear on one horizon while other stars disappear below the opposite horizon. This effect is visible over short distances, which suggested that Earth is not very large. Aristotle estimated the planet's diameter and came within 50 percent of the correct value.

Earth's shadow on the moon showed Aristotle that the planet was spherical.

the future Alexander the Great. After Philip was assassinated in 336 BCE, Aristotle returned to Athens. There, in 335 BCE, he established a school of his own, called the Lyceum. It was also called the Peripatetic School, because Aristotle was in the habit of lecturing while walking in the garden. After Alexander died in 323 BCE, Aristotle moved to Chalcis (modern Khalkis) on the island of Euboea, his mother's birthplace. He died there in 322 BCE.

Aristotle's Teachings

Aristotle's teachings survive in works on philosophy, logic, politics, biology, physics, meteorology, and cosmology. They remained the basis of formal logic until the 19th century. His attempts to explain weather phenomena greatly influenced the study of meteorology.

Aristotle was most successful as a biologist. He observed more than 500 animal species and classified them into hierarchies. He divided animals into those with blood and those without,

TIMELINE

44 BCE–8 CE

KEY:

Engineering and Technology

Astronomy and Math

44 — **44 BCE** Astronomers in China and Italy report a red comet; the color is caused by ash from an explosion of a volcano.

30 — **30 BCE** Syrian craftsmen learn the technique of glassblowing, which is taken up by the Romans.

28 — **28** Chinese astronomers begin keeping records of sunspots, which they continue until 1638 CE.

approximately coinciding with the distinction now made between vertebrates and invertebrates.

Animals that give birth to live young head Aristotle's hierarchy, followed by those that lay eggs, those that produce eggs that hatch internally, those that lay eggs that are fertilized externally, those that reproduce by budding, and finally animals that arise spontaneously from slime or putrefying matter. From this arrangement, Aristotle compiled a "ladder of nature," which remained the basis of animal classification until it was overturned in the 18th century.

Aristotle's View of Matter

Aristotle accepted the prevailing theory of his time that all matter is composed of the four elements: earth, air, water, and fire. But he added a fifth element, "aether," from which he thought the heavens are made. Aristotle believed that Earth, and heaven were subject to different laws. On Earth, everything is corrupt, meaning that it is changeable and liable to decay. The heavens, are permanent, unchanging, and perfect.

Aristotle realized that dolphins are more closely related to land animals than to fish.

19 Roman general Marcus Agrippa orders the building of a 13-mile (21-km) aqueduct to bring water into Rome.

10 King Herod the Great of Judea uses concrete blocks to build an open harbor at Caesarea in Palestine.

1 CE Chinese mathematician Liu Hsin introduces decimal fractions.

8 CE Horizontal waterwheels are used in China.

19 | 10 | 1 CE | 8 CE

Archimedes

Archimedes is considered to be one of the greatest mathematicians of all time. His inventions brought him fame that survives to this day.

Archimedes was said to have discovered one important theory while taking a bath.

TIMELINE

15 CE–77 CE

KEY:

Life Sciences

Engineering and Technology

Astronomy and Math

15 CE An Italian physician, Thaddeus of Florence, describes the uses of alcohol in medicine.

30 CE Aulus Cornelius Celsus writes the first Latin treatise on medicine.

50 Greek mathematician Hero of Alexandria describes a simple steam turbine built as a novelty.

50 The Romans introduce Mediterranean vegetables to western Europe, including garlic and onions.

This illustration shows Archimedes testing the purity of gold in King Hieron's crown.

Timeline

287 BCE Archimedes born in Syracuse

270 BCE King Hieron becomes king of Syracuse; he later asks Archimedes to discover whether his crown is pure gold

c.250 BCE Archimedes screw pump

c.215 BCE Romans lay siege to Syracuse; Archimedes designs weapons to defend the city

212 BCE Siege of Syracuse ends; Archimedes killed by a Roman soldier

Archimedes (c.287–212 BCE) was born in Syracuse, Sicily (then a Greek colony). He studied in Alexandria, Egypt, where his teacher was a former pupil of Greek mathematician Euclid. His studies completed, Archimedes returned to Syracuse, where he remained for the rest of his life.

Levers and Screws

Archimedes was the first person to work out the principle underlying levers. He said that if he had somewhere to stand and a lever long and strong enough, he could move the world. King Hieron asked Archimedes to move a very heavy

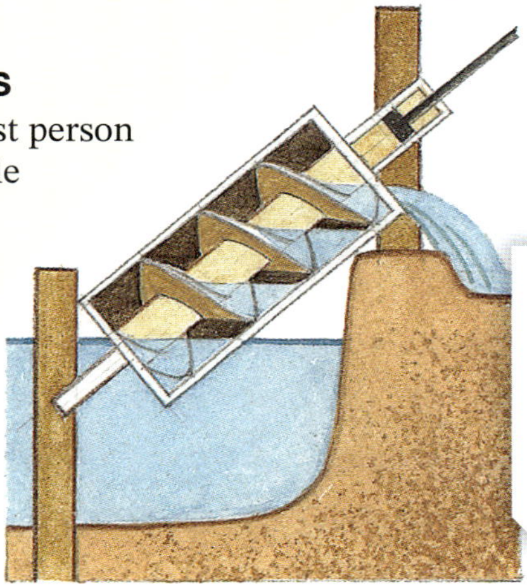

An Archimedes screw pump is angled so that the tip of the tube is in the water. With each turn of the handle, water rises over each thread of the screw until it flows out of the tube's upper end.

62 Hero of Alexandria writes *Metrica (Measurements)*, describing calculations of area and volume.

77 Roman scholar Pliny the Elder writes his 37-volume *Natural History*, summarizing Roman knowledge of the natural world.

62 77

77 Greek physician Pedanius Dioscorides writes *De Materia Medica*, a catalog of drugs and herbs that remains authoritative for 1,700 years.

With the aid of various machines devised by Archimedes, including the fearsome "claws," the city of Syracuse held out against the Roman siege for three years.

object. Archimedes is said to have responded by assembling a system of levers and pulleys with which Hieron himself was able to pull the royal ship *Syracusa* across dry land.

Archimedes is said to have designed the screw pump to irrigate crops (the Egyptians may actually have had this much earlier). It is a spiral screw inside a cylinder that raises water. The system is still used today. Archimedes also helped defend Syracuse from a Roman siege in 215 BCE. The inventor came up with several novel weapons including the "claws of Archimedes," said to pick up and shake enemy ships, and a mirror that focused the sun's rays to set fire to enemy sails. Such weapons held the Romans at bay for three years.

TIMELINE

80 CE–128 CE

KEY:

Engineering and Technology

Astronomy and Math

80 CE The Colosseum is completed in Rome.

83 CE A Chinese writer describes an early form of compass, probably used for divination rather than navigation.

100 Chinese farmers introduce the tandem hitch, allowing two horses, one in front of the other, to pull plows and carts.

80 | 83 | 100

Scientific Investigation

It is impossible to say whether Archimedes really built all the machines that are credited to him. He only published his mathematical work, and saw himself as primarily being a mathematician. He calculated a value for pi that is very close to the modern figure, and devised methods for calculating the volume and surface area of a body with a curved surface. He also developed a way to express very large numbers, demonstrating it with a calculation of the number of grains of sand that exist in the universe.

Archimedes' Principle

When Hieron got a new crown, he asked Archimedes whether the gold was mixed with silver. When Archimedes' bath overflowed, he saw that an object in water displaces its own volume. He is said to have run around shouting *"Eureka!"* ("I've got it!"). He used the method to compare the volume of the crown with that of the same weight of gold. Silver is bulkier than gold, so when the crown displaced more water than the gold, it showed that the king had been cheated.

The Romans took Syracuse in about 212 BCE. The general, Marcellus, ordered that Archimedes should not be harmed. A Roman soldier found Archimedes working on a mathematical problem and demanded that he accompany him. Archimedes told the soldier not to disturb the circles he had drawn in the sand. Becoming impatient, the soldier killed the great mathematician.

Archimedes is said to have used a mirror to beam light at ships' sails to set them on fire.

100 The wheelbarrow appears in China, where it is used to carry goods and people.

105 A Chinese court official describes a way of making paper using tree bark, rags, and other materials.

110 In Greece, Menelaus of Alexandria introduces spherical geometry.

128 The Pantheon, a Greek-style temple, is built in Rome with a 142-foot (43 m) dome made of concrete.

100 105 110 128

Military Technology

Warfare was a regular occurrence in the ancient world. The need for improved weapons and defensive armor led to some important technological advances.

Archaeological evidence suggests that organized warfare existed about 10,000 years ago. This was a period in which people began to live in settlements and develop agriculture. Local skirmishes grew into greater conflicts as different groups of people fought each other to protect themselves and their land. By the time people began making written records, about 5,000 years ago, warfare was common between cities or states.

With the discovery of Earth's minerals and elements, early humans began to make weapons from copper and bronze. These were replaced with the discovery of iron. The Hittites of ancient Egypt are thought to have been the first early humans to use iron weapons. Iron was harder than bronze. Iron swords had sharp cutting edges, and the points of iron spears were more effective at penetrating armor.

A Greek hoplite soldier of the 5th century BCE. He carries a spear and a large round shield, and is wearing heavy defensive armor.

TIMELINE

132 CE–190 CE

KEY:

Life Sciences

Astronomy and Math

132

132 CE Chinese astronomer Zhang Heng builds a primitive planetarium to show the movement of important stars.

140

140 CE Greek physician Aretaeus of Cappadocia describes many diseases and their treatment, including pleurisy and epilepsy.

A bronze hoplite helmet with cheek protectors.

As weapons improved, so did defensive equipment. It was understood that head protection was essential for warriors, and helmets were made from metal. Metal armor for the lower legs, known as greaves, and breastplates molded to the shape of the body or more loosely fitting garments made from iron rings (chain mail) were also introduced. The most critical defensive tool, however, was the shield. In some armies this was often large and covered much of the body.

Roman Weapons

The Roman army was equipped with best in early weapons technology. At its height, the army's infantry soldiers, legionnaries, were armed with standardized equipment. They had spears for throwing, the pilum.

Timeline

10,000 years ago First evidence for organized warfare

1274 BCE In the Battle of Kadesh, Egyptian forces take on the Hittite army in a chariot battle

1200 BCE Iron Age technology develops in the Middle East

800 BCE Assyrian cavalrymen use short bows from horseback, fighting in pairs; one man holds the reins of two horses while the other man fires his bow

100 CE The Roman army is at its peak, using standardized equipment including segmented armor, a large curved shield, a throwing spear, and a heavy short sword

150 The Greek geographer Ptolemy compiles *Almagest*, a digest of ancient knowledge of astronomy. It remains a standard work until the Renaissance, 1,300 years later.

175 Galen of Pergamon, a Greek physician, begins taking the pulses of patients to aid diagnosis.

185 Chinese astronomers observe a supernova (they call it a "guest star") in the constellation Centaurus.

190 Chinese mathematicians express large numbers as powers of ten (e.g., 10^4 = 10 to the power 4, or 10,000).

150 175 185 190

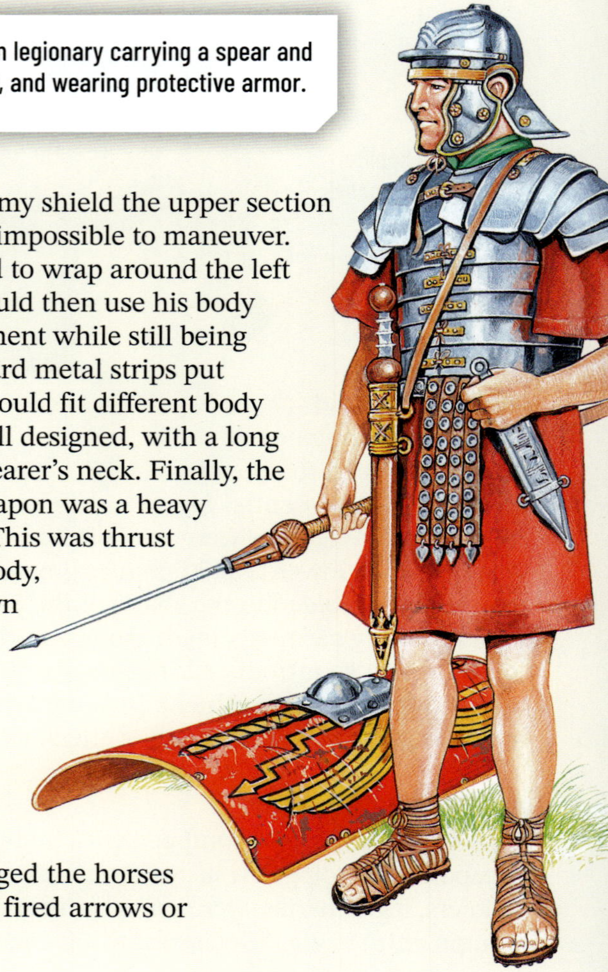

A Roman legionary carrying a spear and a sword, and wearing protective armor.

The pilum had a sharp point. When it lodged in an enemy shield the upper section bent, making the shield almost impossible to maneuver. The Roman shield was designed to wrap around the left side of the soldier's body. He could then use his body weight to push against an opponent while still being protected. Roman armor was hard metal strips put together in segments so that it could fit different body shapes. The helmet was also well designed, with a long back extension to protect the wearer's neck. Finally, the main close quarters fighting weapon was a heavy short sword called the gladius. This was thrust up into an enemy's soft lower body, rather than using it to hack down through helmets or armor.

Chariots

The use of horses became increasingly effective in warfare. The Hyksos invaders introduced chariots pulled by horses to Egypt. A driver managed the horses while one or two other soldiers fired arrows or threw spears at the enemy.

TIMELINE

200 CE–271 CE

KEY:

- Life Sciences
- Engineering and Technology
- Astronomy and Math

200 CE The Moche of coastal Peru build two huge terraced platform tombs from molded adobe brick, dedicated to the sun and the moon.

226 CE Built mainly on arches, the Aqua Alexandrina aqueduct carries water 14 miles (23 km) into Rome.

250 Greek mathematician Diophantus is credited with inventing algebra.

250 Parchment replaces papyrus as a writing material in the Mediterranean region.

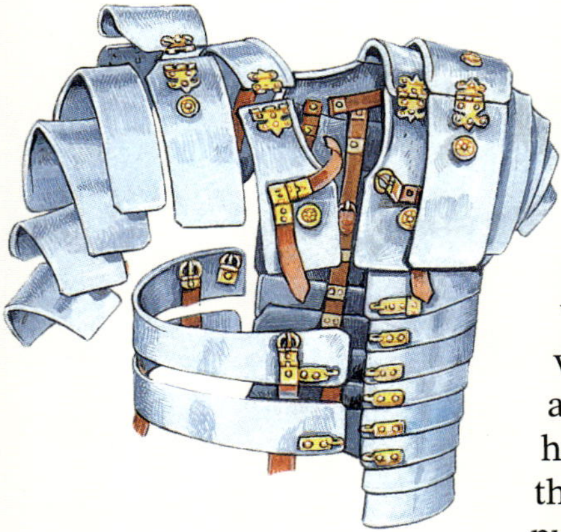

Roman segmented armor held together with leather straps.

Distance Fighting

Weapons that could kill at a distance were also developed. Wooden bows and arrows were improved by using horn and animal glue to increase the tension when the bow was pulled back, so increasing its power and range. In China, archers used crossbows that were extremely powerful and accurate.

A Roman catapult, effective at shooting spears and large rocks or bolts at the enemy.

Projectile Weapons

Siege weapons that could fire spears, rocks, or other missiles were also devised, partly to attack walled towns and cities. Roman projectile weapons used two scientific principles. One was tension, pulling back a single beam then releasing it, so converting potential energy into kinetic energy. This hurled the missile at speed over considerable distance. The Romans also used the principle of torsion. The Roman ballista catapult had two long arms that were pulled back to create tension on thick, tightly twisted ropes. When the "bow" was released, a shallow bowl at the end of an arm propelled a heavy weight toward enemy walls.

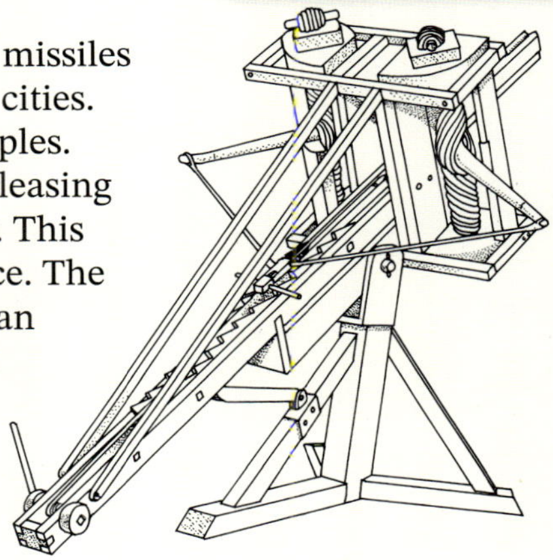

265 Chinese physician Huang Fu Mi writes a major treatise on acupuncture.

271 A compass is used in China for navigation; it is probably a piece of lodestone that indicates the direction of south.

265 269 271

269 The famous library at Alexandria is damaged when Queen Zenobia of Palmyra attacks Egypt.

Roman Roads and Aqueducts

From the fourth century BCE, the Romans built roads throughout their sprawling empire, replacing mud tracks with sophisticated stone roadways on solid foundations.

The three-tiered Pont du Gard was built to carry water to the French city of Nîmes.

TIMELINE

300 CE–400 CE

KEY:

Life Sciences

Engineering and Technology

Astronomy and Math

300 302 310 330

300 CE The Romans notice that the British burn coal as fuel, and soon adopt the practice.

302 CE A Chinese pottery figure seems to show a horseman using metal stirrups.

310 Chinese astronomer Chen Zhuo combines the maps of previous astronomers into a single comprehensive star map.

330 Chinese astronomer Yu Xi describes the precession of the equinoxes, first discovered by the Greeks in about 150 BCE.

Workers building a road. Some clear the roadbed and build curbs, while others lay stones as a foundation for the surface pavement.

Timeline

312 BCE The Via Appia (Appian Way) is the first Roman road

c. 25 BCE Vitruvius sums up Roman knowledge of engineering in his book *De Architectura (On Architecture)*

20 BCE The Pont du Gard is built in France on the orders of the Roman general Marcus Agrippa

80 CE The Colosseum is completed in Rome

122 CE Construction begins on Hadrian's Wall in the north of Britain

At their peak, Roman roads totaled over 50,000 miles (80,000 km) of highways—enough to stretch twice around the world. Roads spread out from Rome in Italy, Lyon in Gaul (France), and London in Britain. In North Africa, roads ran along the coast of the Mediterranean Sea.

The first Roman road was the Via Appia (Appian Way), built southward from Rome in 312 BCE by Roman general Appius Claudius Caecus. Other roads soon followed, such as the Via Aurelia to Genua (Genoa) and the Via Flaminia to the Adriatic coast, each named after a different Roman dignitary.

Parts of the Via Appia are still visible in Italy.

350 An Indian account of astronomy, the *Surya Siddhanta*, is published at about this time.

350 The Chinese begin to cultivate tea plants.

365 The first Western reference to mechanical cranks appears in a Greek text.

369 Chinese astronomers observe a supernova that remains bright for five months.

400 The Chinese begin to use the umbrella for protection from the sun and the rain.

400 Scholars in Alexandria use the Arabic term *al-kimiya* to describe changes in matter; it later gives rise to the words "alchemy" and "chemistry."

350 365 369 400

Hadrian's Wall was a 73.5-mile (118 km) long fortified barrier that helped control the northern frontier of Roman Britain.

The Romans built roads mainly for officials and merchants. But they were also useful for moving troops rapidly in times of trouble. Wherever possible, the roads followed a straight line set out by surveyors using a sighting staff called a groma. Fast chariots could achieve up to 75 miles (120 km) a day on the roads; freight wagons covered 15 miles (25 km) a day. However, as the Roman Empire crumbled, so did its roads owing to a lack of maintenance. Later road builders often took over the routes, as can be seen by the straight stretches of highway on a road atlas of England.

Water for the Cities

As Roman towns and cities increased in size, there was an increasing demand for water for drinking and bathing; public baths and fountains were features of many Roman towns. To bring in the

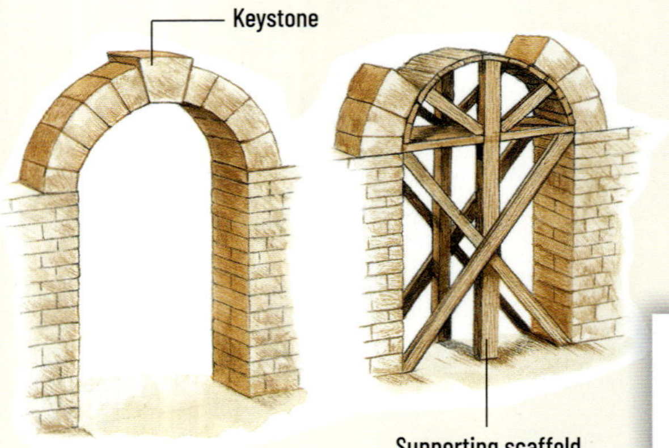

A scaffold supported an arch while it was being built, and a central wedge-shaped keystone locked the final structure in place.

TIMELINE
405 CE–497 CE

KEY:
Engineering and Technology
Astronomy and Math

405 CE Chinese craftsmen make iron stronger by combining wrought and cast iron.

410 CE Greek mathematician Hypatia invents a hydroscope for measuring the density (specific gravity) of liquids.

415 Indian engineers use iron chains to build suspension bridges.

water, Roman engineers built aqueducts. An aqueduct is any permanent channel for carrying water.

Between 312 BCE and 200 CE, engineers built a total of 11 aqueducts to carry water into Rome, some from over 56 miles (90 km) away. The aqueducts sloped very gradually—only a few inches in every mile—so that the water flowed along by gravity. Some Roman aqueducts in Italy, Greece, and Spain are still used today. They include the aqueduct at Segovia, Spain, which is made from 24,000 granite blocks fitted together without mortar in a series of 165 arches. The three-tiered arches of the famous Pont du Gard near Nîmes, France, extend for 900 feet (275 m) and reach a maximum height of 165 feet (50 m). It was built in about 20 BCE by general Marcus Agrippa (63–12 BCE). Both examples are still in full working order.

Stages of Road Building

Roman highway engineers first dug drainage ditches about 40 feet (12 m) apart, then cleared a trench between them, which they filled with sand, mortar, and a series of stone courses as the foundation. They topped the road with stone slabs or cobbles set in mortar. On marshy ground, the whole road was raised above the land. Some major roads had stone curbs 8 inches (20 cm) high and 2 feet (60 cm) wide on each side, with side lanes outside them.

The Colosseum, Rome's great amphitheater, was completed in 8 CE.

465 | 489 | 495 | 497

465 Chinese mathematician Tsu Ch'ung Chi uses a circle 9.8 feet (3 m) across to calculate pi to 10 decimal places: 3.1415929203.

489 Chinese artists carve 165-foot (50 m) statues of Buddha into a rock face at Yungang.

495 A Chinese writer describes a paddleboat with several paddle wheels along each side.

497 Aryabhata, the Indian mathematician and astronomer, proposes that Earth rotates on its axis.

Glossary

alloy A blend of one metal with another to give it special qualities, such as resistance to corrosion or greater hardness. Common alloys include bronze, brass, and steel.

astronomy The study of objects outside Earth's atmosphere.

bronze A hard, durable alloy made mostly of copper and tin.

cuneiform The wedge-shaped writing used in Mesopotamia from the third to the late first millennium BCE.

distaff A rod on which yarn is wound.

domestication The use of selective breeding to adapt wild plants or animals to make them more useful to humans.

eclipse When two celestial bodies are lined up so that one blocks the light of the sun from the other.

hieroglyphics A system of writing, originating in ancient Egypt, which uses pictures to symbolize words.

hunter-gatherers People who follow a way of life based on hunting wild animals, fishing, and gathering berries, seeds, and wild food plants.

irrigation The watering of crops by artifical means, such as canals.

lodestone A naturally magnetic mineral.

lunar month The period of time from a full moon to the next full moon.

ore A mineral from which a metal can be extracted.

papyrus A writing material used by the ancient Egyptians, made by beating together the stems of certain reeds.

peripatetic Somone who walks around.

philosopher A person who studies and tries to explain beliefs and concepts.

plow An agricultural implement that is pulled by an ox, horse, or modern tractor to cut, lift, and turn soil to prepare it for planting crops.

smelting Extracting metals from mineral ores by heating them to high temperatures.

solar year The length of time the sun takes to return to the same position in the cycle of seasons.

ziggurat A temple of rectangular stone tiers (larger at the base and smaller at the top) with an outer covering of baked mud bricks.

Further Information

Books

Alexander, Heather. *Egyptology*. Black Dog & Leventhal, 2021.

Gurstelle, William. *The Art of the Catapult: Build Greek Ballistae, Roman Onagers, English Trebuchets and More Ancient Artillery*. Chicago Review Press, 2018.

Hill, Stuart. *Ancient Wonders Then and Now.* Lonely Planet Kids, 2018.

National Geographic. *Everything: Stone Age to Iron Age*. National Geographic Kids, 2021.

Woods, Michael and Mary B. Woods. *Machines Through the Ages. From Furnaces to Factories* (Technology Through the Ages). Lerner Publishing Group, 2024.

Woods, Michael and Mary B. Woods. *Agriculture Through the Ages. From Silk to Supermarkets* (Technology Through the Ages). Lerner Publishing Group, 2024.

Websites

bigthink.com/tag/ancient-technology/
Big Think resource page with many links to pages about ancient science.

www.britannica.com/technology/history-of-technology/The-urban-revolution-c-3000-500-bce
The history of technology in the ancient world, with links and illustrations.

opentextbooks.clemson.edu/sciencetechnologyandsociety/chapter/the-ancient-world-and-sts/
Science, Technology, and Society, a student led exploration of science in the ancient world.

www.snexplores.org/article/lets-learn-about-ancient-technology
An online resource for students with links, videos, and information that explores all aspects of science in the ancient world.

Publisher's note to educators and parents: Our editors have carefully reviewed these websites to ensure that they are suitable for students. Many websites change frequently, however, and we cannot guarantee that a site's future contents will continue to meet our high standards of quality and educational value. Be advised that students should be closely supervised whenever they access the internet.

Index